The Lost Tooth

By
Laura W. Eckroat

Illustrated by
Greg White

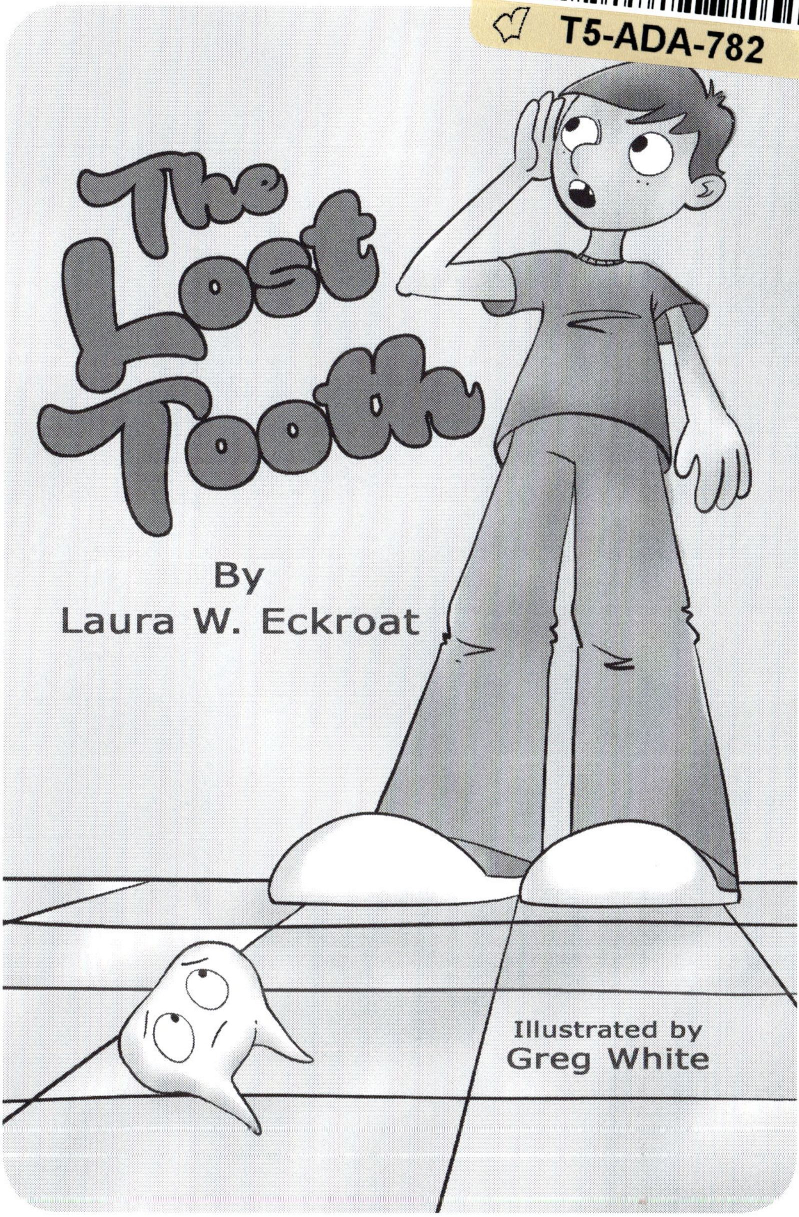

Kidspiration Junior Chapter Book Series #1

Copyright 2017 by Laura W. Eckroat
All rights reserved.

No part of this book may be reproduced in any form or by electronic means, including information storage and retrieval systems, without written permission from the publisher, except by a reviewer, who may quote passages in a review.

Published by Crescent Renewal Books
An Imprint of Who Chains You Publishing
P.O. Box 581
Amissville, VA 20106
www.WhoChainsYou.com

Illustrations by Greg White

ISBN-10: 1-946044-15-6
ISBN-13: 978-1-946044-15-0

Printed in the United States of America

First Edition

KIDSPIRATION

William:

Thank you for inspiring me to move out of my comfort zone and write in a way I haven't written before!

My Kidspiration series are stories inspired by children I have met through my years of teaching and writing. In this series I will use higher level words in the stories to help children learn new vocabulary. Kidspiration stories are words of encouragement and life lessons from children who have KIDSPIRED me.

Also by Laura W. Eckroat

A Simpler Time

Daisy, A Life Cycle Series

The Life of Bud

Went Out to Get A Donut,
Came Home With A Muffin

What's In The Corner:
A Muffin "Tail"

Contents

Chapter 1: Crush, Squash, Pulverize.......................... 1

Chapter 2: Unhinged.. 7

Chapter 3: Alone and Afraid...................................... 9

Chapter 4: The Dustpan 11

Chapter 5: Clean up 15

Chapter 6: Here We Go Again................................. 18

Chapter 7: Lost.. 20

Chapter 8: Found?... 26

Chapter 9: Now Where Am I? 29

Chapter 10: The Pillow 30

Chapter 11: Morning Surprise................................. 33

Laura W. Eckroat

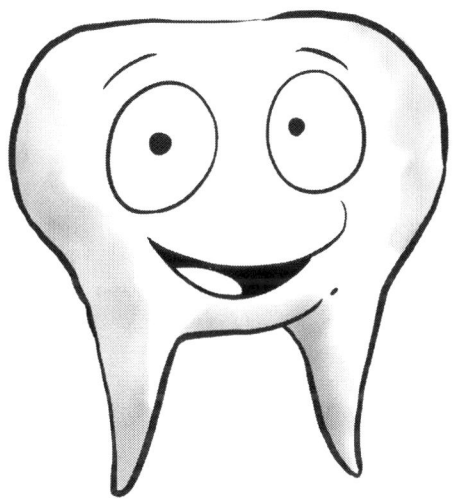

Chapter 1:
Crush, Squash, Pulverize

Hi! My name is Tommy, Tommy Tooth. I have many friends, 19 to be exact. My closest friend's name is K-NINE—his bark is much worse than his bite! My life is pretty good, I get to hang out with my friends every day. Even though we are **stationary**, we do keep busy many times throughout the day.

It will be all quiet, then, when we least expect it, the fun begins—we get to CRUSH, SQUASH, and PULVERIZE all kinds of interesting textures! We've demolished hard and sugary things,

The Lost Tooth

slurped slippery and cold items, consumed soft and sticky stuff, and devoured so many other interesting substances.

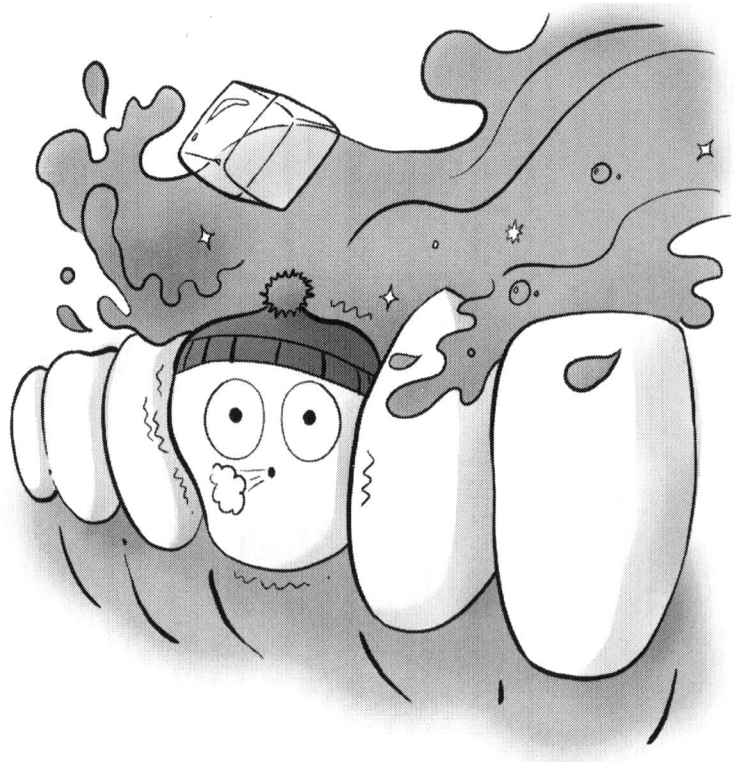

We are small, but we are always up for the challenge.

I must admit, I live in a very strange place. Most of the time it is dark and kind of spooky. There are long periods of time we are all in the dark and we do absolutely nothing.

Laura W. Eckroat

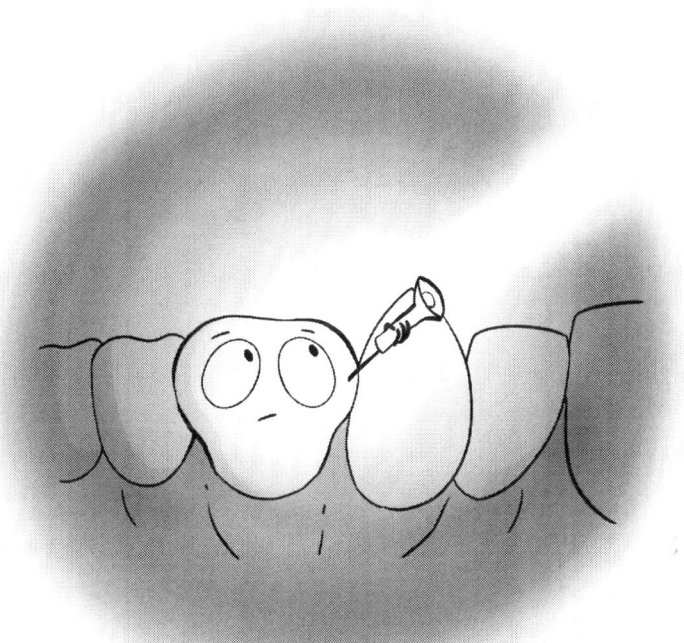

Just when **complacency** sets in, a huge **crevice** opens and crazy things start happening!

The Lost Tooth

A couple times a day a minty string swipes both sides of me with lots of force and leaves me feeling smooth and clean. Water swishes all around me and then with a sudden burst, it is gone.

But, my favorite part of the day is when this bristly brush lathers me up with foam! The bristles gently scrub every side of me, the foam is tingly, and I feel like someone cares about me.

Laura W. Eckroat

But lately, I've been a little off my game. For the last few days I've felt a strong push from below me. I've tried to push back but I am just too little and apparently not as strong as I thought. I am trying to ignore the pushing, but it is really making MUNCHING difficult!

Every time I begin to CRUSH, I wiggle and jiggle. At first it was just a little wiggle but now it is a LOT of jiggle. Every time I try to CHOMP and MASH, I begin worming and squirming all over the place. I feel like I am going to become unhinged!

The Lost Tooth

WHAT IS HAPPENING TO ME!!!

Laura W. Eckroat

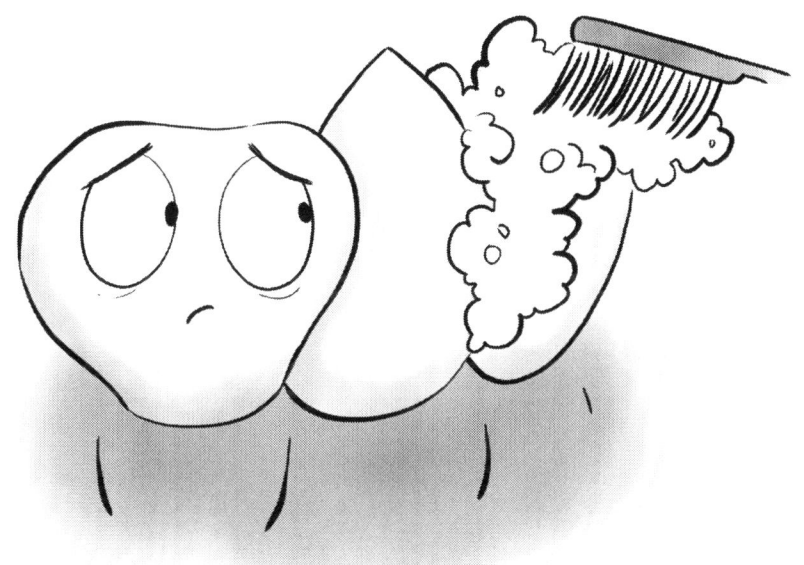

Chapter 2: Unhinged

Today, when the cavern opened and the string was doing its thing, it didn't even touch me. When the water was sloshing around me, I felt dizzy. As the foam rushed by, the bristles left me alone. I felt sad ... why was I being ignored?

As I was **pondering** my **predicament**, some crunchy flakes came my way. As I began to

The Lost Tooth

SMUSH them, I suddenly found myself being tossed around in a sea of white creamy liquid and crushed up flakes. Just when I thought life couldn't get any odder, I was thrust out of the only home I have ever known by the giant pink squishy that lived beside me for so many years.

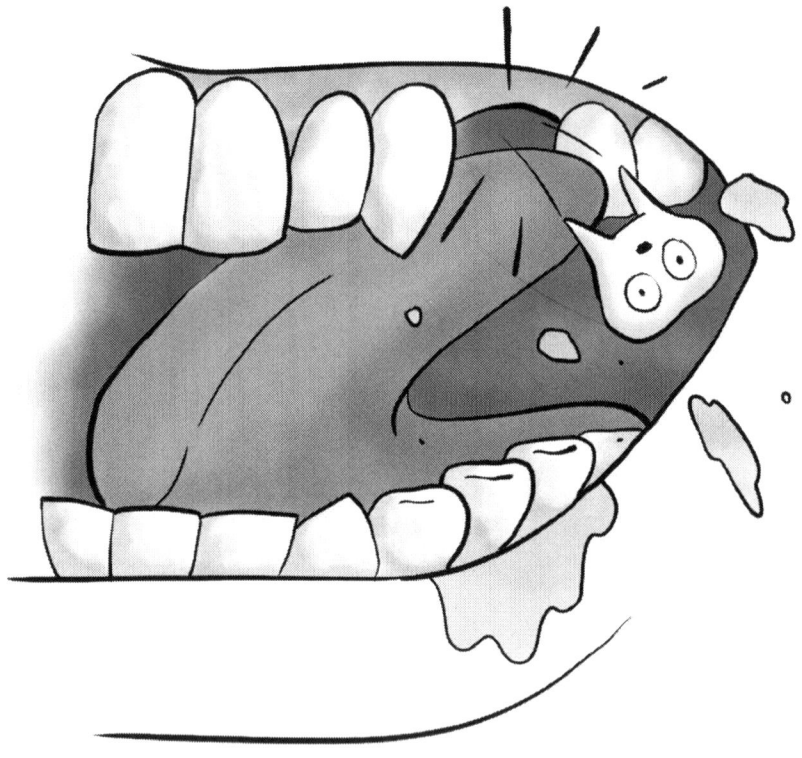

Laura W. Eckroat

Chapter 3:
Alone and Afraid

▲

I tumbled and tumbled for what seemed like an **eternity**—which is a really long time! Then, with a sudden jolt, my journey came to an abrupt stop. I landed in a small pool of liquid, covered in mushy flakes. I did not know

The Lost Tooth

which end was up. None of my friends had joined me and I felt completely alone. I was not standing upright anymore; I was on my side and couldn't move. I tried to yell for HELP, but realized that without my friends, the giant pink squishy, and the cavern that opened and closed, I made no sound. When I settled down, I came to understand that I was underneath some kind of machine. The machine made a soft humming noise that was quite relaxing. So, I just laid there—and waited and waited and waited.

Laura W. Eckroat

Chapter 4: The Dustpan

▲

My surroundings were now dark and dusty, very different from what I was used to. Well, I was used to the dark, but I missed being showered with water every few minutes and really missed K-NINE, too. I began to think that the string and bristles and foam were all a

The Lost Tooth

dream. I was waiting for the "fun" to begin, but nothing happened—there was no CHOMPING or SQUASHING or PULVERIZING. My world was now quite boring.

As I lay there, I heard a voice I recognized ... it was calling out for me. "Toooooooooth, where are youuuuuuuu???" After awhile, I heard another sound that made me even more upset. The words calling out for me were mixed with sadness and tears. I felt there was no hope; I realized this may be my new home —F O R E V E R!

I was feeling sorry for myself, I admit, when I was stunned back to reality by a GIANT brush that swooped me to the side. I was caught in a whirlwind of dust and what appeared to be some sort of fur. I recognized one of my past acquaintances—a pasta noodle—except last

The Lost Tooth

time I saw him he was squishy. This one was stiff.

Next thing I knew we were whisked onto a pan and were being touched by what looked like an octopus to me. I was flicked to the left and to the right and then the octopus thing grabbed me and lifted me up off the pan! I am not going to lie, at that moment fear is all I felt. Where was the octopus taking me?

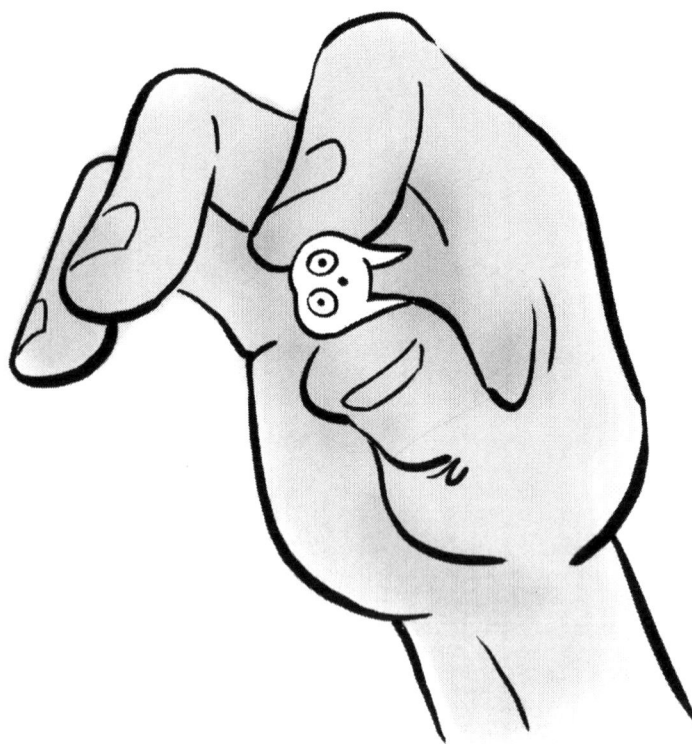

Laura W. Eckroat

Chapter 5: Cleanup

▲

"I found your tooth," yelled a lovely-sounding voice. Squeals and laughter followed. The octopus held me tightly and I was drenched by some cool water that felt wonderful! I was once again clean, and

The Lost Tooth

was gently placed on a soft, damp, spongy surface. "Let's leave the tooth here, where it's safe. Tonight you can place it under your pillow," said the lovely voice.

So that is where I stayed.

My thoughts drifted and I remembered how it all began. When I first emerged into the cavern, I would gently GNAW on plastic toys and tiny fingers and the occasional teeny toes. As time marched on, a tiny rubberized spoon would fill the cavern with creamy delights in crazy colors like green, orange, and purple.

Over time, my friends kept popping up and we all worked together as a team: CRUSHING, MUNCHING, and PULVERIZING.

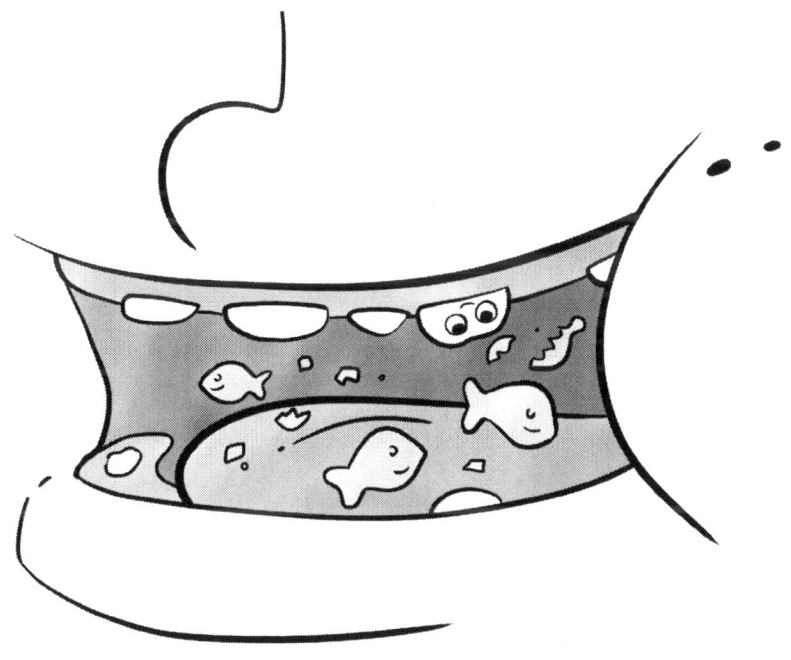

We started out with easy things like crackers shaped like small fish and moved on to bigger challenges like lollipops and pretzels.

Lying on the spongy surface was very strange; I wasn't sure what was going to happen and I wondered how long I would be there. I also had no idea what a pillow was and why I was going to be placed under it!

The Lost Tooth

Chapter 6:
Here We Go Again

▲

I was jolted from my thoughts when a frantic voice bellowed "the dog spilled water everywhere, get a towel!!" Immediately my world was rocked once again. The damp, soft,

18

spongy surface was whisked out from under me and I found myself sailing through the air.

This time when I hit the hard surface I rolled for a bit before I came to what seemed to be a peaceful stop, nestled in between some cushy fibers.

Could this be a pillow? I soon figured out—it wasn't.

The Lost Tooth

CHAPTER 7: LOST

▲

For days I was trapped in the cushiness of fuzzy strands that stood straight and tall. Giant things kept going right over me, pushing me deeper into the fibers. I kept hearing a forlorn voice saying, "We'll never find it, my first tooth is lost forever." With each passing day, I sunk deeper and deeper into the cushy place and deeper and deeper into **despair**.

I truly was a L O S T tooth. When I thought I would never be saved I heard a loud whirring sound. It was getting louder and louder and seemed as if it was coming straight at me. The sound was deafening and a very bright light was shining on me. I felt like a lone performer on a stage! I thought someone or something might be coming to rescue me.

The Lost Tooth

All of a sudden my new "friends"—the dust bunnies and the dirt devils—were sucked upwards and magically vanished! I WAS TERRIFIED!!!

I found myself being pulled upwards with such force I could do nothing but go along for the ride. I was twirled around this bristly brush and whisked through a long, dark tunnel. I became tangled in a debris field so creepy I couldn't think straight. I heard a faint voice say, "Oh no

… what was that?"

The loud sound stopped and the dust and dirt settled. It became eerily quiet. I laid there in a mound of dirt, dust, hair, string, and other strange small pieces of who knows what.

Next thing I knew, I was being flipped around and landed on a smooth, cool surface. The octopus was lingering over me again, and snatched me from the pile of dust.

The Lost Tooth

"Here you are! William will be so excited."

Once again I was bathed in cool water, but this time I was placed in a small see-through holder. The sweet voice said "You should be safe in this glass."

Uncertain of what might happen next, I had nothing to do but wait.

Laura W. Eckroat

The Lost Tooth

CHAPTER 8: FOUND?

▲

Now that I was "found", I wondered if something other than dust and dirt was in my future. I wished something magical would happen. Just as I was dreaming about better days, a joyful voice screeched, "Thank you, Mom, for finding my tooth!!"

I banged the side of the glass and was jostled and jiggled and, once again, airborne. As soon as I hit the floor, this big, black, wet, sniffer was nudging me around and I was being lifted back up into the air. I found myself stuck to the black, wet sniffer, which was proving to be quite a thrilling experience.

Shrill voices were yelling "Bandit, nooooooo!!" The furry creature, whose name must have been Bandit, started racing through the house. I had a front nose seat and felt like an outlaw on a horse in an old western being chased by the sheriff.

The Lost Tooth

The house was full of laughter and cheers, and this made me feel full of life too for the first time in a long while.

My exciting ride came to an abrupt stop as Bandit bumped into a large, soft object. I gently slid off his nose and found myself "sitting" in a big, comfy chair.

A deep, friendly voice exclaimed, "William, your tooth's right over here, on the chair. Come get it and let's take it to your room right away."

Laura W. Eckroat

Chapter 9: Now Where Am I?

▲

A very small octopus picked me up and gently hugged me. The tiny octopus wrapped me, like a present, in a very soft cloth. I couldn't see and could barely hear anything, but I felt safe. A soft, tired voice said, "Let's get you to the pillow."

The Lost Tooth

Chapter 10: The Pillow

▲

The package I was in was squeezed tightly by the tiny octopus, and I heard gentle footsteps going up ten stairs. I remembered this familiar sound from my days in the cavern. I was placed on some sort of surface, and I heard the drowsy voice quietly whisper, "I'm so glad we found you. You need to go home to the Tooth Fairy, especially since you are my first tooth. I never gave up on you and hope you have many more adventures!"

I then heard water running and bristles scrubbing. I hoped my old pals were enjoying the brushing and swishing. When the water stopped flowing, I was picked up again and was lovingly placed on a very soft mat. I felt a big, soft, squishy rectangle settle on top of me. I felt safe and at peace. The sweet, sleepy voice said, "Goodnight, Tooth." And then, all was quiet.

I laid there for quite some time in the soothing dark place, but then felt as if I was being transported somewhere else. When I was unwrapped, I was greeted by a small being with wings. I realized this must be The Tooth Fairy!

She welcomed me and told me that my journey had not ended, but had just begun. She explained how I would now wait patiently for my friends to arrive. Someday, we would all be

The Lost Tooth

placed in a new home, with a new child, and then we'd be Munching and Crunching and Pulverizing again! She told me to enjoy my time here and relax as much as I could.

I asked The Tooth Fairy if she would do me a special favor. I explained what I wanted to do, and she said, "Most certainly, I'll deliver it tonight."

Chapter 11: Morning Surprise

▲

The next morning, William woke up and immediately looked under his pillow. He found a little book called **The LOST Tooth**, along with 2 quarters. He was thrilled! Inside the book was a handwritten note in the most beautiful, fancy writing.

William grabbed the book, money, and note and went flying down the stairs to his mom. "Mom, look what The Tooth Fairy left for me!"

The Lost Tooth

Mom looked at the book and money and said, "Wow, you're a lucky boy, Son!"

Then William said, "Mom, can you read me this note?"

Mom looked a bit confused, replying, "William, where did this come from?"

William told her, "The Tooth Fairy left it for me."

Mom took the note and slowly began to read it:

Dear William,

Thank you for giving me that first nudge that pushed me out of my comfort zone and into the big wide world. I've experienced adventures that have had their ups and downs, but you've given me inspiration to try new things and see where my path leads me. My journey was sometimes scary and I'm sure my future will have some bumps, but thanks for never giving up on me. I am now safe and sound with The Tooth Fairy, who will watch over me while I get ready for my next chapter in life.

Good luck in your next chapter, too.

Thanks again,

Tommy Tooth

Mom stood there stunned, in silence. William ran off with his book and money and note. He took the note and put it under his pillow, to remind him to never give up on anyone and to always encourage people to take a chance.

William sat down in his reading chair and called to his little sister Maya. Maya came bounding joyously into William's room and plopped herself down in the cushy bean bag. With his sister cuddled next to him, he slowly opened the front cover and began reading her his very first Chapter Book.

Learning to use higher level words in writing is EXCITING! Here are a few you can use next time you write a story....

GLOSSARY

▲

Complacency: *NOUN.* Unaware or uninformed of dangers or deficiencies.

Crevice: *NOUN.* A narrow opening.

Despair: *VERB.* To lose all hope or confidence.

Eternity: *NOUN.* Infinite time, lasting forever.

Pondering: *VERB.* To think about, reflect upon.

Predicament: *NOUN.* A difficult or trying situation.

Stationary: *ADJECTIVE.* Standing still, not moving.

Kidspiration: *NOUN.* Giving an adult or one of your friends some inspiration to do something they are afraid to do or try.

About the Author

Laura W. Eckroat is the author of *A Simpler Time, Daisy: A Life Cycle Series, The Life of Bud, Went Out to Get a Donut, Came Home with a Muffin,* and *What's in the Corner? A Muffin "Tail."*

Laura was born and raised in Whiting, Indiana. She has lived in Colorado, Georgia, Massachusetts, and Texas. She now resides in Wisconsin with her husband, Steven, and their two rescue dogs—Muffin and Shadow.

Mrs. Eckroat is an elementary school teacher, and a lifetime Chicago Bears football fan. She enjoys gardening, reading, writing, and doing fundraisers for dogs.

About the Illustrator

Greg White's passion for visual storytelling led him to the field of illustration, and he now works as a freelance artist and illustrator, specializing in children's books, comic books, and poster design.

He resides in Oklahoma City, where he has illustrated over 200 books, including the New York Times bestseller, *It Starts with Food.*

Greg attended Southern Nazarene University, where he received a Bachelor's degree in Mass Communication.

Also by Laura W. Eckroat

Went Out to Get a Donut—*Came Home With a Muffin* is a happy-go-lucky, singalong story of adopting a pup named Muffin. The colorful illustrations by Greg White perfectly complement a wonderful tale that will engage our smallest readers while teaching love for our companion animals.

WHAT "MUFFIN" LOVERS ACROSS THE COUNTRY ARE SAYING ...

"Went Out to Get a Donut *is a fun book to read to your child while at the same time introducing the importance of adopting and rescuing animals. Mrs. Eckroat helps start the conversations with this book."*—Sherwin Daryani, Executive Director, Operation Kindness, Carrolton, TX

About Crescent Renewal Books

★

Crescent Renewal Books is an imprint of Who Chains You Publishing, and spotlights uplifting or educational books in all genres.

We hope you enjoyed this book by author Laura W. Eckroat, and will consider reviewing *The Lost Tooth* on Amazon, Goodreads, or other sites. Your reviews mean the world to our authors, and help them expand their audience and their voice. Find links to *The Lost Tooth* and all our Crescent Renewal books through our tab on our website at whochainsyou.com.

Made in the USA
Lexington, KY
09 October 2017